Written by:
Alyssa Wilburn

Illustrated by:
Tabitha Hamm

My Teacher's a Chicken!

To order additional copies of this book, contact:
Xlibris
844-714-8691
www.Xlibris.com
Orders@Xlibris.com

ISBN: Softcover   978-1-6641-2362-5
        EBook   978-1-6641-2361-8

Print information available on the last page

Rev. date: 08/28/2020

Teacher popped through the doorway with a loud "What are you doing?" Her sing songy voice gave us a jump!

"Teacher, you're like a chicken. You just popped out of nowhere!"

"If I was chicken, I would go bawk, bawk. Bobbing my head back and forth."

All our friends laughed.

"Teacher, you're not a chicken, you're a dragon!"

"If I was a dragon I would breathe fire and ROAR!"

"No! No fire, you breathe water. And lions ROAR!"

"Teacher, Teacher! You're a giraffe because you're so tall. You can almost touch the sky!"

"No, not a giraffe.
You're a wolf."

"If I was a wolf I would howl
at the moon, owooooo!"

"What if I waddled around the classroom from side to side?"

"You look like a penguin! They move like this."

"You take care of us
and give us hugs!"

The End

About the Illustrator

Tabitha Hamm always had a love for drawing for as long as she could remember. She attended Grand Canyon University where she graduated with a bachelor's of Digital Design with an emphasis of Animation. She is inspired by her peers and family and her favorite thing to draw is all things mythical. She has illustrated a variety of books ranging from travel laws to children mathematics education. She is always looking forward to learn something new!

Printed in the United States
By Bookmasters